The Study and Teaching of the English Bible

Being Four Lectures

By
G. CAMPBELL MORGAN, D.D.
At Westminster Friday Bible School

Revised for Press by
E. DUNSCOMBE DE RUSETT, M. A.

Wipf & Stock
PUBLISHERS
Eugene, Oregon

Wipf and Stock Publishers
199 W 8th Ave, Suite 3
Eugene, OR 97401

The Study and Teaching of the English Bible
Being Four Lectures
By Morgan, G. Campbell
ISBN 13: 978-1-59244-604-9
ISBN: 1-59244-604-3
Publication date 3/17/2004
Previously published by Fleming H. Revell Company, 1910

INTRODUCTION

IN this series of lectures I propose to deal only with the first and fundamental matters, as my purpose is preëminently that of helping those who are beginning the Christian life in the study and teaching of the English Bible.

Among English-speaking people there are two classes likely to read the Bible; first, those who are Christian believers, and secondly, those who, as honest enquirers, are desirous of knowing exactly what is taught in the Scriptures.

There is a distinct difference between these classes in the *mood* of approach, and consequently in the *mode* thereof. The first almost necessarily comes to the study of the Bible with a prejudice in its favor, expecting to find therein teaching which will guide in life and service; while the second approaches the study with a perfectly open mind as to what the Scriptures teach, but in many cases with a prejudice against the attitude of the first, not being prepared to admit upon the basis of the conviction of others, that the Bible is the Word of God, that it is a Divine Library, or that the writings are in any special sense inspired. Such a reader does not believe these things because he honestly cannot, and is not prepared to make his judgment blind. There are many senses in which such an attitude is the most easy to deal with, for it is the true condition for receiving teaching.

These classes are, however, unified, by their common desire to study the Scriptures; and they are both asking for help as to the best method of doing so.

It would appear as though there ought to be no difficulty in the matter, but it is quite certain that there is a very serious difficulty. This difficulty is the result of the way in which the Bible has been treated, rather than the outcome of anything in the Bible itself. There are thousands of people who have been brought up in somewhat close relationship to the Christian Church, who nevertheless think only of the Bible as a book of texts from which sermons are preached, or which are quoted in proof of some theological position. The result is an entirely false conception of the value of the Scriptures, and is largely to blame for the present condition of affairs. As I have travelled on both sides of the Atlantic, endeavoring to teach the Bible, and striving to help men to a methodical study thereof for themselves, I have been constantly asked by intelligent young people, some of them decided Christians, others honest enquirers, Will you tell us how to study the Bible?

Now I have never been asked to tell any one how to study Shakespeare. That may be accounted for by the fact that no one suspects me of any ability in that direction; but I venture to say that it is a question that is not asked, even of those who are Shakespearean experts; and the reason is that Shakespeare has not been submitted to the false treatment which the Bible has received; and consequently the difficulty and perplexity have not been created.

The present lectures are intended in the simplest way possible to answer that enquiry.

Outline

THE STUDY OF THE ENGLISH BIBLE

I

SOME PRELIMINARY CONSIDERATIONS

A. As to the Bible.	B. As to the Study.
It is :—	It requires :—
I. Religious.	I. Honesty.
II. Dual.	II. Reverence.
III. Triple.	III. Diligence.
IV. Multiple.	IV. System.
V. Unified.	V. Response.

FIRST let me speak of some purely elementary matters which are necessarily preliminary to Bible study. There are certain matters we must understand before we open the Book, and these are set out in brief form in the accompanying diagram. It will be seen that there are two main divisions, the first dealing with preliminary considerations as to the Bible; and the second with the preliminary considerations as to the study thereof.

A. As to the Bible

I. *It is religious.*

It will at once be conceded that it is necessary to recognize that this is essentially a Library of religious literature. It may incidentally contain scientific facts, or philosophic principles; but it is neither a scientific textbook, nor a philosophic treatise. The nature of its declarations are all primarily religious. They are declarations concerning God and man, and the interrelationships between them.

For the present I am not concerned as to whether the teaching is true, for that is not at all the question at this point. We do not start with that assumption. For the moment I am simply insisting upon the fact that, whether true or false, it is a literature of religion; it claims to declare the truth about God, the truth about man, and the truth about the relationship between God and man.

That it is religious literature is also clearly evident when we consider not merely the nature of its declarations, but also the nature of its appeal. That appeal is twofold, consisting of a call to faith in God, and of a demand that such faith shall be demonstrated by works. That is the double message of the Bible from first to last. If at the moment this may appear to be a narrow conception of the Biblical message, it may be well to say that any decision as to the narrowness or breadth thereof must be postponed until the teaching has been examined.

And yet it must at once be conceded that the effect which this Book has produced, and still does produce, compels the recognition of the fact that it is religious literature. This effect is twofold—spiritual and moral.

It is spiritual in that it produces a belief in the life which lies beyond the present. Wherever men have come to this Bible, have been diligent students of it, and have obeyed its first and simplest calls, following in the path of obedience as its teaching has been more completely understood, they have invariably become spiritually-minded, that is, conscious of the reality and vastness of those facts and forces which are not discernible by the natural senses.

If there may be objection to the fact or

value of this position, the moral effect produced by the Bible is beyond question. It is true that there have been those who have declared that they discovered immoralities and indecencies in the Bible; but the answer to such a statement is that no man, woman, or child has ever come to the honest study of this Book, pure in thought and intention, and been made immoral thereby.

Therefore, we must admit that the Bible is religious in the best sense of the word, because of the effect it produces; and it is well that we at least calmly enquire whether it is conceivable that an untrue book can produce the result of truth; or a base look produce results so full of nobility of conduct and of character.

II. *It is dual.*

Turning to the more technical matters, it is necessary to recognize that the Bible consists of two parts which we describe as the Old and the New Testaments, or Covenants. The former consists of a collection of the sacred writings of the Hebrew people, and the latter a collection of the sacred writings of the Christian Church. At the moment we are not concerned with the subject of the fixing of the Canon of either of these parts. That is a question outside the scope of the present lectures. I am simply dealing with the Book as it stands.

In the Old Testament we have the complete sacred writings of the Hebrew people, as they existed in the time of Christ, although not arranged in exactly the same order. It is the same collection of books as were gathered together in the Greek version which we describe as the Septuagint, and which was certainly in existence two or three centuries before Christ; and which moreover is of great interest and value to us because nearly all the New Testament quotations were made therefrom.

In the second part we have the sacred writings of the Christian Church, that is, the writings which the Church has accounted sacred, and has separated from other books because they have peculiar value in that they set forth the fundamental principles of the Christian religion.

III. *It is triple.*

Each of these two parts has three principal qualities: historic, or statements concerning the past; didactic, or teaching for the government of the present; predictive, or foretelling of the future.

In the Old Testament we have the history of the Hebrew people; an account of their origin, their destiny, their failure; and all this principally on the side of the Divine method of dealing with them. This Hebrew history is prefaced by a brief statement concerning the first things in the history of the human race.

In the New Testament the history deals with one Person, Jesus of Nazareth, and with about sixty or seventy years of the movement resulting from His presence in the world.

The didactic portions of these two divisions consist of teachings which appealed to the times in which they were given. In the Old Testament we have, side by side with history, a body of prophetic messages delivered to the people. These teachings, however, have a wider application than that to the age in which they were delivered, for they contain fundamental principles which have abiding values. It is necessary, however, to remember that in the study of these writings it is only such principles which are of abiding value. We are not to-day to go back under the Mosaic or prophetic economy, and if we limit our morality by the narrow and imperfect outlook even of the finest Hebrew thought, we shall sadly fail.

When we come to the New Testament we find teachings which are applicable to the whole period which commenced with the advent of grace, and will end with the advent of glory. Everything which those who have believed in the one Lord and Master need for the government of individual life, the organization of the corporate Church, and the work of the proclamation of the evangel to the world, is found in these writings.

The predictive element in the Old Testament is very remarkable, consisting of prophecies foretelling events, some of which have already been fulfilled, and some of which are not yet fulfilled. In the New also we have definite predictions, some of them from the lips of the one central Person, the Lord Jesus Christ, and some from the pens of those who were His followers. Many of these predictive writings are full of mystery; some of them have been fulfilled, while others await fulfillment.

These three elements are found, I repeat, in each part of the Divine Library, and we must recognize them, or we shall find ourselves in endless difficulty in our study. If we treat history as prophecy, or prophecy as history, confusion is inevitable. Before reading any book we need to recognize whether its character is historic, didactic, or predictive.

IV. *It is multiple.*

Each part of the Divine Library consists of a collection of writings. In the Hebrew Scriptures we have thirty-nine books (there were not quite so many in the form in which the Hebrews had their Bible, because certain which are now counted as two appeared therein as one), and these were written by about one-and-twenty authors. I purposely leave the number indefinite, because it is not established, for instance, who wrote the Book of Jonah, or Kings, or Chronicles; and in our present study our appeal can only be made to internal evidence.

In the New Testament we have twenty-seven books, written by ten writers, that is, if we admit that Hebrews was not written by Paul. If it be admitted that he wrote it, then we have only nine authors.

Thus we have sixty-six books from the pens of some thirty different men, and their writing extended over a period of at least fifteen centuries. Between many of these there could have been no possible collusion, and it is of great importance that in the commencement of our study we remember this multiple character of the Library.

V. *It is unified.*

Finally, it is necessary from the commencement to recognize that the whole Library is unified in a Person. A man taking up these books and reading them might not immediately discover this fact; but it would be hardly possible for an honest and careful student to fail to do so ultimately. At this point, however, I think it well that those who are beginning to study should accept the practically unanimous testimony of those who are well qualified to give such testimony as the result of long and earnest attention to the Library, that the books are unified in the central Person presented.

In the first division, that of the sacred writings of the Hebrew people, there is a constant movement towards, and expectation of, the coming of One who is to be a Deliverer. It is true that the vision is not always equally clear. Sometimes the thought seems to centre upon a nation as fulfilling the idea, then upon a remnant out of a nation, and again a Person is definitely and distinctly expected. Sometimes, perhaps almost unconsciously to the men who wrote or sang, the nation idea is lost sight of, and that of a remnant passes out of sight, and there comes into clear relief the figure of one superlative Person. Everything in the sacred writings of the Hebrew people leads towards this One, sighs for Him, and is conscious of imperfection apart from Him.

In the first five books there is a record of the search after a priest; in the historic writings we have the quest for a king; while in the didactic portions we hear the sigh for a prophet. Nevertheless in the whole of these books we fail to find perfect priest, or king, or prophet; notwithstanding the fact that the idea of each has been borne in upon the mind, and the necessity for such is evidently the supreme conviction of the unified teaching. In brief, the sacred writings of the first division consist of a literature revealing a people who in their religion, their history, and their ideals are making a pilgrimage, in the light of a hope which remains unfulfilled.

When we turn to the New Testament, the sacred writings of the Christian Church, we find what Carnegie Simpson has so happily described as the Fact of Christ. The historic section consists of five books, the first four of which tell the story of His presence in the world; while the fifth describes the first movements in human history resulting from that presence. The didactic portion consists of the writings of those who were His followers, and explains more fully the mystery of His Person, and the resources and responsibilities of His people. The predictive element throughout has to do with His final triumph.

Thus, while in the Old we have a progress towards a Person, inspired by a hope, in the New we have a process from a Person, inspired by a fact. Thus, the whole Library is unified in this one Person.

Now it is conceivable that these Hebrew people may have been deceived, and that this Christian movement may have resulted from imagination. I am not at the moment concerned with these matters, but rather with the attempt to recognize the nature of the literature. Whether rightly, or wrongly, at the centre of the Bible is a Person, and its first division sets forth the history of a people searching, seeking, and sighing after Him; and the second presents Him, and the things resulting from His presence in the world.

Therefore we cannot demolish any part of the Library without the whole suffering. That whole stands or falls together around the unifying fact of the central Person.

B. As to the Study

I. *It requires honesty.*

It is preëminently necessary that we come to the study of this Bible without prejudice either for or against it. I do not desire to undervalue the prejudice in its favor in the case of many, which results from early training. My own first acquaintance with the Bible was distinctly, and I am constrained to add, graciously, influenced by this prejudice. My earliest reading of the Book was a reading in a frame of mind prejudiced in its favor because of what it was to my own father and mother. But while I thank God for these things, yet the Book never became truly my own until I dared to face it apart from that prejudice, and allowed it to deliver its own message to mind and heart and will.

It is a grave mistake to demand this prejudice in favor of the Bible from a class, or an individual student, when its very existence may prevent the honest and profitable study of it.

At the same time, it is absolutely unfair to come to the Bible with a prejudice against it. It must be treated honestly by being approached with an open mind, and for this purpose it is not required that any special view of inspiration be held. We ought to come to the study, determined to set aside our prejudice in its favor, and our prejudice against it, and our prejudice against the prejudice of those who believe or do not believe in its Divinity. I earnestly plead for this open mind, believing that wherever the Book is given its opportunity of producing its own impression, it will win a singular victory.

II. *It requires reverence.*

Since we must admit our limitation of knowledge concerning the subjects with which the Bible professes to deal, we ought most reverently to listen to what it has to say. To take the superlative instance of the existence of God, there are necessarily so many things which we do not know about God, that we ought to listen reverently to anything which claims to be a declaration concerning Him. Our very ignorance demands that as we listen to what the Bible has to say about Him, we should do so with reverence. This is true of all the themes with which it deals. They are high and superlative themes, and therefore, whether the statements be true or false, we ought at least to give reverent attention.

This need for reverence is further emphasized by the convictions which the very best men of the centuries have held concerning it. No man of a few brief years of life has any right ruthlessly to trample underfoot the convictions of centuries, and imagine he can deal flippantly with a literature which has produced such convictions. It seems to me that whatever conclusion I might ultimately arrive at concerning this Book, I could never consent to deal irreverently with pages made sacred by the fact that my own father pored over them in life, and at last pillowed his head in death upon their statements, and passed out of sight in perfect peace because he believed them to be true.

III. *It requires diligence.*

Two words will suffice to convey what is in my mind as to the diligence which is demanded of those who desire to be students of the Bible: intensity, and continuity. Any person desiring to study such literature ought to give the best he can of time and attention to the work. The Bible should be studied when the mind is freshest and most acute. Continuous study is also necessary; the patient persistence which avoids hasty decision, and is content to work and watch and wait. I do not hesitate to affirm that the Bible demands more diligence than any other literature.

IV. *It requires system.*

No man is in any sense a Bible student who takes up the Bible and reads it by a method which can only be described as haphazard. To open it at a page and read, to take a certain portion allotted for each day by others, may be perfectly justifiable methods for pleasure, and may result in profit; but they do not constitute study, in the true sense of the word. The system should be from general to particular, from extensive to intensive. Personally, I should advise any one commencing the study of the Bible to begin at the centre, and work to the circumference, to commence with the Gospel narratives rather than with Genesis. All that will be considered more particularly in subsequent lectures; but the general principles of a true system is that of first gaining a knowledge of broad outlines, and then concentrating upon details.

V. *It requires response.*

Religion is primarily volitional, and I now affirm that it is impossible to read this Book without being conscious that it makes appeal to conscience and to will. Whenever it does that, when it captures the conviction, the student must respond by obedience, or it inevitably becomes a sealed book. Such a statement may seem to contradict much that I have said as to the open mind; but I am compelled to make it, because it is demonstrated true by the constant and unvarying experience of those who give themselves to this study. I personally believe that the reason why many people have lost their love for the Bible is that they have failed to recognize the necessity for obedience to its moral claims. The first conviction that possesses the soul of the truth of some Bible teaching, clamors within the conscience for the yielding of obedience thereto, and if we fail to obey, the light will fail. Knowledge unmixed with obedient faith is not only profitless, it is harmful. The student must approach the study of this Book in that attitude of mind which says, "If it speaks to me, I will obey."

II

THE FUNDAMENTAL PROCESSES

A. Activity.			B. Result.
I.	Survey.	Read.	Impression.
II.	Condense.	Think.	Outline.
III.	Expand.	Work.	Analysis.
IV.	Dissect.	Sweat.	Knowledge.

WHEN we turn to consider the fundamental processes of Bible study, it is well that we distinctly understand that we are dealing with the study of the English Bible, and not with the Scriptures in the original languages, that being another subject altogether, although in order to an understanding of the books, the same methods might with advantage be followed in dealing with the Hebrew and Greek documents.

By fundamental processes I mean those which will enable us to come to an accurate knowledge of what these books contain. I refer to them for the moment as books, because I am growingly impressed with the importance of beginning with the Bible as a library, rather than with its unity as a book; a library having two parts, three qualities, and a multiplicity of writers, themes, and dates—a true library.

I may also first of all state three things with which I do not propose to deal, because they are outside the scope of our present consideration, these being preliminary to them.

First, then, the fundamental processes do not deal with the veracity of the books. That is necessarily considered in the study of introductions. The question of authorship and authenticity does not occur in the fundamental processes.

Neither have they anything to do with the arrangement of Biblical teaching into the form of systematic theology. This is final rather than fundamental. I hold that every man should test his systematic theology by his Bible, rather than his Bible by his system of theology. In this connection I remember a quaint but illuminating story of a negro preacher, to whom Dr. Broadus, the great Baptist theologian of the Southern States of America, gave a volume of his commentary on the Scriptures, saying that he hoped it would be useful to him in his work. Some time after the reception of the gift, Dr. Broadus again met the preacher, and enquired whether he had found the commentary helpful, and the reply was, "Oh, yes, Massa, it is a berry good book; but there is one thing I have noticed about it." "What is that?" enquired Dr. Broadus. "Well, Massa, it is that the Scriptures do throw a lot of light on it." That I believe is true of many of our theological systems; and therefore, from my standpoint, it goes without saying that Bible study is preliminary to any attempt to systematize theology.

In the third place, the fundamental processes do not include the application of the Bible to all the details of practical life. This again is a final matter.

Of course these fundamental processes must affect the final processes, and in the study of the Bible we are ever approaching a systematic view of truth, and always finding application of the things we discover to the actualities of every-day life.

It is impossible to study these books in the way I am going to suggest, without some impression being made upon the mind as to their veracity; without coming to definite conceptions concerning God and man, and the interrelationships between them; without hearing an appeal to conscience, and having a constantly growing conception of what conduct ought to be at its highest and its best.

Nevertheless, we are to consider the first things in Bible study; those which we must undertake before we decide whether the book is true; before we attempt to systematize our theology; before we can make accurate application of its teaching to life and conduct.

Personally, I am convinced that there is a true *order* in these fundamental methods, which I have attempted to indicate in the diagram at the commencement of this chapter; showing also what the *activity* is in each case; and what the *result* produced will be.

In the first process we survey; in the second we condense; in the third we expand; in the fourth we dissect. Having followed these processes we may adopt any other methods we please, and shall do so the more intelligently as the result of this preliminary work.

I believe that it is well to postpone the discussion of the veracity of any book until we have given time to it along these lines. We have no right to say that any book is untrue, or even that it is true, until we have taken time for these methods of examination. If any one is tempted to say that it will be impossible for us to complete the study of the Divine Library by these processes in a lifetime, let me frankly say that I am in perfect agreement; but at the same time it is well to remember that, apart from these processes, we shall never know any given book in the Library. Many great Biblical scholars and earnest saints have given their life to the work of Bible study, but none has succeeded in working through all these processes in the case of more than a few books.

Once again, let me, even at the cost of wearisome repetition, repeat that these processes are fundamental; and that those which follow will become clear and forceful in the proportion in which we have adopted them.

A. Survey

This means *reading;* and results in an *impression.*

In commencing our study it is well that we bear in mind the principles set forth in the previous lecture; and whatever book we take, we should first define its place in the Library; as to whether it is a Hebrew or a Christian document; and also its quality; whether it is history, teaching, or prediction. The activity in order to survey is that of reading. It is necessary first, to decide to take practically no notice of the chapter and verse divisions which we find in our ordinary Bibles. They all have their uses for reference, but they may sadly mislead us in our attempt to gain a general impression of a book. Let the book be read straight on, and in reading *look*, *listen*, and *live.* Look closely at what you are reading; listen to what the words you see are saying; and live for the time in the very atmosphere which is being created by the reading of your book. Some one may say, who has given more time to study other literature than the Bible: "But that is exactly what you would do with any book!" Certainly; and if men will begin to read the Bible with the same common sense as they employ in the reading of other books, they will be on the highway to an apprehension of its meaning, which hitherto they have lacked; and that statement explains the reason for my suggestion that the reader should forget the chapter and verse divisions. Who would consent to any other literature being subjected to this mechanical method of division? I remember that eminent Bible scholar, and wonderful teacher, Dr. Henry Weston, once saying in my hearing, "I hate these chapters and verses; reading a Bible in which I find them always reminds me of riding over a corduroy road." He was an old man, and remembered the first roadways in the Western parts of the country, and how that the logs of which they were formed were so laid that in travelling over them one experienced a series of bumps which were neither conducive to speed nor ease; and that is exactly the mental effect produced all too often by reading a chapter divided into verses, one experiences a series of jerks. There is great value in Dr. Moulton's Modern Readers' Bible, simply because he has arranged it in literary form, omitting the chapters and verses.

Having read the book, read it again; and in the same way. Then read it once more. After that read it again; and yet again, until you become conscious that the book has made an impression upon your mind; that you have a conception of its general movement. That is the first process. In the course of the reading make a note of special phrases or words that occur repeatedly, or of any particular thought which seems to be insistent.

I may illustrate what I mean by saying that such reading of the Book of Numbers produced upon my mind the impression of a people on the margin of the land, about to enter it, turned back to a long period of wandering, after which they came again to the margin of the land, with the result that the general outline of the book for me is always connected with that impression, and is so tabulated. As I have repeatedly said in dealing with this subject in public, I think my analysis of books are the result of having read them on an average from forty to fifty times. Some, of course, yielded an impression more quickly, while others took many more readings. That will often depend upon the individual. There are books which may produce a clear impression upon the mind of one man far more quickly than upon that of another. Therefore, we do not accept any man's analysis as final; but it is well to observe this law of reading a book over and over again until we know it, not by rote, but by an impression of its purpose clearly stamped upon the mind.

B. Condense

This means *thinking;* and results in an *outline.*

The book having thus been read through again and yet again, and an impression having been made upon the mind in the way I have indicated, the attempt should now be made to express in the briefest way possible the contents of the book. This means quiet thinking over what has been read, accompanied by reference to certain parts in order to clear statement.

Now will be found the value of the things noted in the course of reading, the recurring words and phrases, and insistent thoughts. The first result of this process will be the statement of the content in the fewest words possible. Here I may illustrate by saying that if I were asked to put Genesis into three words, I should do it thus, Generation, Degeneration, Regeneration.

The next process is the reading of the book again, only now in the recognition of the general divisions suggested, and that in order to change, adjust, abandon, and perhaps to find a new and better brief outline.

The mind being settled about the general

outline, these main divisions should be treated in the same way, and subdivided into sections.

At this point in the process it is well to make use of every book which is likely to help, until we arrive at what seems to us to be a satisfactory outline. It is not until this has been done that we are ready for the next stage.

C. Expand

This means *work;* and results in an *analysis.* Of course, I can only illustrate what I mean from work which I have done. Therefore let me instance the Book of Matthew. In constant reading of this book I do not think it is possible to escape the impression produced by the recurrence of the word *began* on two outstanding occasions (see iv. 17 and xvi. 21). Now the impression made upon the mind by the survey of Matthew is that we have been in the presence of a King.

The outline gained when we condense is, that Matthew presents the Person of a King; tells the story of the propaganda of the King; and finally leads us into the presence of the Passion of the King. So far we have a mere outline.

Now we may turn to the expansion of that outline, and in order to do so we need to sit down quietly with each of these sections, and carefully work for the production of an analysis.

There must first be grammatical analysis, the taking of each section, paragraph by paragraph, with determination to discover the principal sentences, and to note the grouping around them of subordinate sentences, and the interrelationships between these.

This, of course, is specially necessary in studying the Pauline epistles, in which by reason of the Apostle's constant turning aside, we are in danger of missing the principal affirmation of passages under consideration.

I cannot too earnestly urge the importance of studying the Bible thus analytically, and of refusing to abandon a passage until its real sense is understood.

In the course of this work let us be most careful not to mutilate a passage simply because at first we do not comprehend its meaning; or in an endeavor to escape difficulties.

I may give an illustration of what I mean from those excellent volumes to which I have referred, the Modern Readers' Bible. In the volume containing the Book of Jonah, I am compelled to say that I think I find one of the smartest and most unfair things of this kind that I know. The two statements concerning the fish, one before the psalm of Jonah, and one after it, are removed from the main text, and are inserted as foot-notes. In his notes, Dr. Moulton says: "The reference to the *great fish* prepared to swallow Jonah is in literary form a foot-note exegetical of the expression in the song, 'Out of the belly of hell'; similarly the vomiting out Jonah is a foot-note attached to the last line." Now there is absolutely no warrant for such a statement, other than the conception that the story is not likely to be true, and it is easy to account for an inaccuracy by suggesting that the original writing has been altered, as Dr. Moulton does, by saying that "these particular foot-notes have every appearance of being a gloss or later edition." This method of treating any part of a paragraph which does not square with our philosophy is not fair to the book under consideration. If a passage is difficult, there is all the more reason for patience, persistence, and determination to read and reread until it is understood.

In this process it is more than ever necessary that we should not be in bondage to the chapters and verses, as we find them in our ordinary Bibles. Again, to take a familiar illustration, we entirely miss the beauty of some of the final words of our Lord when we read the fourteenth chapter of the Gospel of John alone. The true beginning of what we find in that chapter is in the previous chapter, and if the concluding words of chapter thirteen be read in immediate connection with chapter fourteen, we have a new light upon our Lord's intention. He was speaking to Peter, and in close connection immediately associated others with him, as He said, first to Peter: "Wilt thou lay down thy life for Me? Verily, verily,

I say unto thee, The cock shall not crow, till thou hast denied Me thrice;" and then without a break, to Peter and the rest: "Let not your heart be troubled: ye believe in God, believe also in Me."

The whole of the section will show that Christ said in effect to this man, "I know the worst that is in you, and that presently you will deny Me; but I know also that I am able to realize the best that is in you, and that if you will trust Me, in spite of all the worst, I shall at last bring you to the place I go to prepare for you."

It is by such careful expansion of our outline by thinking, and examination, that we come at last to the possession of a detailed analysis of a book.

D. Dissect

This means—to use the word of the hard student in other departments—*sweat;* and results in *knowledge.*

The word "dissect" suggests the scalpel and the microscope; and the idea of the scalpel is warranted by the expression, "rightly dividing the word of truth," which means, correctly disjointing, so as to bring each part into perfect separation.

This is the most fascinating part of Bible study, that to which I personally have never yet been able to give much time or attention, save in the case of a few books. Each sentence is now to be pondered in itself, and in its relationship to all the other sentences. Every word is to be carefully examined as to its root meaning, and as to its use at the time when it was written.

Here, of course, is the place where you need all the help and all the scholarship available. There is a fine and ever-growing exegetical literature for which the true student of the Word is profoundly thankful; and of which he will avail himself to the utmost of his ability.

The work of dissection needs patience and persistence, but it yields the most astonishing results, full of fascination and delight to those who give themselves to it earnestly.

All these processes must be recognized, and

in a measure employed, before any single text can be made the basis of a sermon. To think out a sermon which seems religious, and then to hunt for some Biblical text upon which to hang it, is little short of profane. True sermon-making is in the last process a dissection of a paragraph or text, which has been chosen in recognition of the results of all the earlier processes. When any single passage of Scripture is taken as the basis of a sermon, our first business is to enquire from which part of the Library is the book selected; then in which part of the book; next in which paragraph; and finally, what does it really say?

And in order to discover this, with the light of the surrounding context shining upon it, it should be taken word by word, that the value of each may be known; and then as to its statement, that its true message may be discovered. That, as I understand it, is true preparation for preaching; and consequently, it is evident that the first work of the preacher is that of Bible study, and Bible study by these fundamental processes.

Let no man imagine that such preaching is cheap or easy. The idea that expository preaching can be done without work is entirely false. On the other hand, that is not Biblical preaching which finds a text, and then reads all available books to see what other men have said about it, finally arranging these thoughts into a sermon.

The way to study the Bible is to study the Bible; and to give time and attention to the business; to read, to think, to work, to sweat! These are the requirements, especially of those who profess to teach or preach. If my final words may be spoken to those who are looking forward to the ministry as to a sacred life-work, I would say to them that Bible preaching demands that they give themselves to the study of the Bible with all the powers of their being. When they do so, they will find that the illuminating Spirit of God will lead them into a land of romance, of breadth, of depth, of constant delight. I may be allowed to speak out of my own experience and to say that I can truthfully use the words of the palmists and say:—

"Oh, how love I Thy law!
It is my meditation all the day."

Such study of the Bible inevitably makes appeal to conscience. This literature has volitional values beyond the merely intellectual and emotional. Therefore, at the end of every hour of study, whatever the process may be, that of survey, condensation, expansion, or dissection, let the life be submitted to the truth which has been discovered; and then by all means let there be instant obedience to the shining of the light; for by this method alone can we be prepared for new unveilings; and by this method the Bible will become, as the days go on, more and more full of value, and full of delight.

THE TEACHING OF THE ENGLISH BIBLE

III

THE NEED

A. As to the Nation.	B. As to the Church.	C. The Inter-relation.
I. Conceptions: The Supremacy of the Spiritual.	I. Revelation: The Doctrines of the Faith.	1. Vindication by Realization.
II. Conduct: The Splendor of the Moral.	II. Interpretation: The Laws of Life.	II. Illustration by Manifestation.
III. Character: The Strength of the Unselfish.	III. Inspiration: The Charter of Service.	III. Initiation by Communication.

IN approaching the subject of the teaching of the English Bible, I do not propose to deal with the science, history, or importance of teaching itself. These must be taken for granted.

It is, nevertheless, important that we should recognize that our subject is that of teaching.

Of course, I do not undervalue the work of preaching; but for the moment we must draw a distinction between the two. Preaching is in many senses the greater word, because it includes teaching, while it emphasizes proclamation, interpretation, and application. Our present subject is that preliminary teaching which is the making known of the content of the Bible, and which prepares the way for its interpretation and application.

In dealing with the need for teaching, I propose to do so from the standpoint of one who is a student of the Bible, having accepted the preliminary considerations as laid down in the first lecture, and followed those fundamental processes indicated in the second.

It is well that I should at once say that the result of my acceptation of these considerations, and my following of these processes, is that I believe the Bible to be the Word of God, and it is from the standpoint of that conviction that I speak when dealing with the need of teaching the English Bible.

It may therefore be well to deal a little more

fully with the declaration that I believe the Bible to be the Word of God. It is not enough to say that in this literature there are embodied truths which are found nowhere else save as they have reached other writings from the Bible; that there are quantities here which constitute the message of God, but which we are left to discover from the midst of much which lacks that supreme quantity.

I believe that the Bible is the Word of God. Yet carefully notice what that statement really means. I do not believe that the Old Testament is the Word of God. I do not believe that the New Testament is the Word of God. I do believe that the whole Library constitutes the Word of God to man. As the result of my own study of the different parts of the Library, and the resulting sense of the unity of the whole, I am convinced that presiding over all the human thinking and writing was a Divine mind, safeguarding the expression of thought, so that no words contrary to truth were employed.

The unity of the message is the demonstration of its Divinity. Genesis is not the Word of God. It is a part of it. Genesis interpreted by Revelation—and for such interpretation all that lies between is necessary—is the Word of God. Exodus is not the Word of God; but Exodus and Leviticus interpreted by Hebrews is the Word of God. The law of Moses is not the Word of God; but the law of Moses fulfilled by the grace and truth which came by Jesus Christ is the Word of God.

With such distinction in mind it is impossible to go back to Old Testament history and its morality for New Testament times. Passing through the processes of the Old we find our way to the central Figure, and from there study the interpretation of the New, and thus we are in possession of the Word of God to man.

The question of the Canon is not now before us; but in passing I may say that I believe the Spirit of God, who presided over the thought of the men who wrote presided also over the choice of the Christian Church until in due time the completed revelation resulted.

From these briefly stated views it will at

once be seen how strong my conviction must be as to the necessity for the teaching of this Bible. I propose to speak of that necessity in three ways: First, from the national standpoint; secondly, from the Church standpoint; and finally, from the standpoint of the interrelation between the two.

A. As to the Nation

The matters of supreme importance to the life of a nation are three; its conceptions, its conduct, its character. That is the true order of statement, because it is the order of experience. The final matter in the life of a nation is its character. This is the result of its conduct, and its conduct issues from its underlying conceptions.

I. *Conceptions: The supremacy of the spiritual.*

The inspirational centres of thought are those which are of supreme importance as much in the life of a nation as in the life of a man. What the nation thinks the nation will do, and eventually the nation will be. Ideas are the most mighty factors in national life.

The central, vital conception which the Bible supplies to the nation is that of the supremacy of the spiritual over the material. The Bible assumes the existence of God, and declares His government in all the affairs of this life; it also teaches the eternal duration of man's existence. These being the fundamental propositions of the Biblical revelation, the Bible messages enforce the resulting deductions.

The Bible assumes the existence of God, and insists upon the government of God, who is without beginning or end of days, who is from everlasting to everlasting, in a mystery of being which our minds have never been able to compass, and yet in the consciousness of which we find the only resting-place for the otherwise restless spirit of human enquiry. The opening sentence of the Bible is full of suggestive sublimity, "In the beginning God created," and from that first word to the last the burden of its teaching is that of insistence upon the existence of God. It never explains, nor does it attempt a philosophy which will finally express in the formulæ of human wisdom the fact of that existence; but it affirms it, and insists upon the resulting fact of the government of God.

The Bible teaches the eternal duration of man's existence, and necessarily, therefore, gives to man those spiritual conceptions which compel him to put all the things of the present and passing moment in relation to the abiding ages.

Such conceptions call the nation back from the vain imagination that the dust of to-day is everything, or that the hurried passing hour has in it anything of finality. Such conceptions fling the horizon further back, expand the outlook, give august spaciousness to ideas concerning everything near, because it is seen as intimately related to that which is infinite and distant.

II. *Conduct: The splendor of the moral.*

Such conceptions issue in conduct conformed to a splendid standard of morality, that of conformity to the will of that God who is the Creator and supreme Governor of the universe. The expression of that conformity to the will of God, according to Bible teaching, is that of doing good to other men.

While these matters are condensed into brief sentences they ought to be treated as of supreme importance. To speak of doing good to other men does not mean, according to Bible teaching, that men should refrain from doing to others what they do not desire others should do to them. That is a merely negative and selfish morality which is pagan. The ultimate expression of responsibility in the Bible is contained in the words of our Lord, which we now describe as the golden rule, "Whatsoever ye would that men should do unto you, even so do ye also unto them." That is positive and self-sacrificing. It is often asserted that this golden rule had already been given to men by other teachers; but any comparison of the sayings which are quoted in proof of this assertion will show that they are all infinitely removed from the ethic of Jesus in the way we have indicated. Morality, then, according to the Bible, is, as to its standard, the will of God, and as to its expression, truth and love towards our neighbor. Such morality influences conduct in business, in pleasure, and in friendships. The morality of the Bible is always linked to a spiritual conception. There is a great deal of morality which leaves the spiritual element out of count; but it is weak, anæmic, and useless for the making of a mighty nation. "Happy is the nation whose God is the Lord," because wherever spiritual conceptions constitute the inspiration of conduct the conduct resulting is characterized by a splendid morality.

III. *Character: The strength of the unselfish.*

The character of a nation whose conduct is that of a morality based upon spiritual conceptions is always that of unselfishness. Unselfishness is that submissiveness of tone and temper, resulting from subjection to the throne of God, and His sovereignty, which expresses itself in the service of other men. All the graces and virtues which we admire in our own nation and in the individuals which compose it, whether they be kings, princes, lords, or commoners, the graces and virtues which even, what we speak of as, the secular press speaks of with admiration, are graces which result from the fact that this nation has an open Bible, and in its deepest heart believes in God. So surely as we lose that open Bible, we shall lose this spiritual conception, this conduct of high and true morality, and this character which is great and strong by reason of its unselfishness.

All of which explains my conviction of the supreme importance in the life of a nation of the maintenance of the teaching of the Word of God.

B. As to the Church

The Divine Library is supremely the literature of the Church, and supplies revelation, the doctrines of the faith; interpretation, the laws of life; and inspiration, the charter of service. The matters of supreme importance to the life of the Church are those of its faith, its life, and its service; and this constitutes the true order of statement because it is the order of experience.

I. *Revelation: The doctrines of the faith.* These are found in the Bible and are of fundamental importance. I once heard Dr. Lyman Abbott declare to a company of theological students that it was important to distinguish between theology and religion; that religion is the life of God in the soul of a man, and that theology is what a man thinks about God. He went on to declare that the supreme matter is religion, and that what a man thinks about God is not of any great importance. While I am prepared to accept his distinctions, and agree as to the importance of making them, I do not accept the deduction. I believe that religion is the outcome of theology. In this application it is true that as a man "reckoneth within himself, so is he."

What, then, are the doctrines of the faith which the Bible presents? As I am now dealing with what I hold to be the need of the teaching of the English Bible within the

Church, I may summarize the doctrines of the New Testament as being those which present the Lord Jesus Christ, Son of God and Son of man, first as Revealer, secondly as Redeemer, and finally as Ruler. These are the central doctrines of the Bible; the hopes, aspirations, and expectations of the Old Testament; the certainties, realizations, and dynamic of the New.

Christ is the Revealer, and it is important that we do not treat that as a narrow conception. He is directly the Revealer of God and of man, and indirectly, but none the less certainly, the Revealer of the devil. He reveals God, so that the conception of God within the Christian Church is the result of what Christ was in Himself. He reveals man, so that our ideal of the possibility of humanity we owe entirely to what He was in His humanity. He reveals the devil by bringing him into the clear light of His own triumph over him, so that with the apostle we are able to say "We are not ignorant of his devices."

Christ is the Redeemer. He not only reveals

God to man, He makes it possible for man to return to Him. He not only reveals to man the possibility of his manhood, He makes it possible for him to be what he ought to be, what it was meant he should be in the economy of God. He not only reveals the devil to man, He leads man in the conflict against the devil, wherein he becomes more than conqueror through Him who loved him.

Christ is the Ruler. Having revealed and redeemed, He becomes the one Lord and Master of those who accept the grace of His redemption, and return to the government of God.

Of course it is at once recognized how condensed a statement this is, no reference being made to what the Bible teaches as to the nature of the revelation, as to the method of the redemption, or as to the programme of the Ruler. I have simply attempted to gather into three of the briefest words the essential facts of the faith—those, namely, that Christ is Revealer, Redeemer, and Ruler. If these doctrines are not named, they are all implied.

The implication of Christ as Revealer is the fact of the Incarnation. The implication of Christ as Redeemer is the fact of His Atonement. The implication of Christ as Ruler is the fact of His Resurrection. In every case these implications must be taken into account when we ponder the revelation of the Bible which constitutes the faith of the Church.

II. *Interpretation: The laws of life.*

Having thus enunciated the doctrines of the faith, the Divine Library interprets the value of that faith as the inspiration of works. We cannot do better in attempting to summarize these laws of life than make use of the inclusive, exhaustive words of Paul in his letter to Titus, when he declared that the grace of God having brought salvation to all men, we should live righteously, soberly, and godly (Titus ii. 11, 12). In these three words every relationship of life is included. "Soberly" has to do with the world *within*, all the hidden fact of personality under control, balanced, poised, strong; no longer swept by passion, but mastered by principle. "Righteously" has to do with the world *around*, the attitude of the Christian towards all other human beings; and the context is illuminative as it deals with the old men, young men, old women, young women, and servants, while other writings deal with other relationships such as those of husband and wife, parent and child, and masters; the whole of which are summarized by suggestion in the word "righteously." "Godly" has to do with the world *above* and *beyond*, the facts and forces of the spiritual universe. Thus the laws of life are those which demand, as to my own life, that I live soberly; as to the world of men with whom I come in contact, that I live righteously; as to the world of spiritual forces, that I live godly.

III. *Inspiration: The charter of service.*

The final value of the Scriptures to the Church is that they provide her charter of service. With regard to this I need only briefly summarize by saying that the Bible teaches that the purpose of her service is the establishment of the Kingdom of God; the programme of her service is obedience to the commissions of the Son; and the power of her service is the indwelling of the Spirit.

The importance of the Bible to the Christian Church if these things be true cannot be overstated. If here we have a literature containing the doctrines of the faith, the interpretation of that faith in the terms of the laws of life, and the charter of service which results from acceptation of the faith, and obedience to the laws, can there be anything of greater importance than that we should study this literature in order to understand our faith, to know the laws of our life, and yield ourselves to service?

C. The Interrelation

The interrelation between the need for the Bible as to the nation and as to the Church is of supreme importance. The final value of Bible teaching within the Church is that it is only as the Church knows this Word of God and proclaims it to the nation in life and service that the influence of the Bible can be exerted in the life of the nation. It is not merely by teaching the contents of the Bible to the nation as such that we can supply its conception, inspire its conduct, or create its character. It is only as the Bible is supplied to the nation through the witness-bearing of the Church, incarnating its teaching, that the nation profits thereby. The fact of this inter-relation therefore creates the responsibility of the Church, and that may be indicated by three words, namely, Vindication, Illustration, Initiation.

I. *Vindication by realization.*

The conception of the supremacy of spiritual things is vindicated in the life of the nation in the measure in which the Church realizes the doctrines of faith. Of course, I use the word "realize" at this point in the sense of making real, not in the sense of comprehension merely. A Church composed of those who know God, are made nigh to Him by redemption, and under the rule of their Lord and Master live in constant obedience to His Kingship, is the Church which compels conviction in the life of the nation of the reality of spiritual forces.

II. *Illustration by manifestation.*

This word touches the realm of conduct, and of course the conduct is that which results from the spiritual conception, and is true to those standards of morality which the Head of the Church enunciated and illustrated in His own teaching and life; the supremacy of the will of God, and the necessity for love and truth in all human interrelationships. The splendor of the moral ideal can only be illustrated in the life of the nation by the Church, as she manifests the life governed by these standards.

III. *Initiation by communication.*

If the word "communication" in this connection is a somewhat startling one, I nevertheless use it of set purpose and most carefully. The unselfish character must be communicated to the nation by the Church, as she is obedient to her charter of service, making the Kingdom of God her perpetual passion, the commissions of the Son her sufficient programme, and the indwelling of the Holy Spirit her perpetual power; she thus initiates in national life the movements which tend to the creation of the unselfish character; and she communicates a virtue which compels national conformity to that character of unselfishness which is the character of abiding strength.

On the chart giving the outline of the scheme of this lecture I have attempted to indicate the connection between the different parts of this revelation of the need for the teaching of the English Bible. The spiritual conception in the nation is related to the faith of the Church by the Church's vindication of the faith by realization. The conduct of the nation is related to the laws of life within the Church by the Church's interpretation of those laws by manifestation. The unselfish character of the nation is related to the charter of the Church's service by the initiation through communication. The Bible must be taught in the Church, in order that it may be taught in the nation; and the interrelation between these two things I have tried to illustrate by this simple diagram.

The Bible is the Word of God, that is, it is the truth for men. Take the Bible from the Church and what happens? The Church is the pillar and ground of the truth, and if it lose the Bible it becomes a lamp without a light, a pedestal without a figure. By such loss the Church is of no use to the nation.

On the other hand, give the Bible to the Church, let the Church know the Bible and love the Bible, then it will be a light and a revelation, and so will be able to fulfill its true function in the national life, and by such fulfillment the nation will be constrained towards spiritual conceptions, moral conduct, and unselfish character.

I have deliberately chosen not to speak in this lecture of the immediate evidences of the need. In conclusion, I may touch in a few brief words thereupon. There is an immediate need for the teaching of the Bible within the Church, first because of its long-continued neglect, and secondly, because of the present urgent enquiry. Of course, there is a sense in which it is true that the Bible has not been neglected. It is found in all the churches of the Christian faith, and in all the homes of Christian people; and it has been read both in the church and at home in certain ways; but if we submit any ordinary congregation of professing Christian people to a simple examination as to the content of the Bible we are almost appalled at the ignorance manifested. On the other hand, the hour is supremely characterized by a spirit of enquiry, and of earnest desire to know what the Bible teaches. It is my profound conviction that wherever men and women are raised up to teach the Bible they will find the people of God eager to hear and to learn.

It is a question whether there was ever graver need than now in the national life for the teaching of the Word of God. The conceptions that underlie our policies are on the whole far from noble. There is much of animalism and of mammon contaminating our thinking; and the moralities in which we are very much inclined to make our boast are after all lowered moralities; and there is in large measure forgetfulness, if not denial, of spiritual inspirations which alone create great morality. As a nation we are not governed by unselfishness of character, but by an appalling and narrow selfishness. It is my personal conviction that the only cure for the things which threaten us as a nation is a new crusade of teaching and preaching the Word of God. That the Church may return to a study of that Word which shall issue in the incarnation of its teaching in order to the salvation of the nation is the one dominant need of the hour.

IV

THE METHOD

A. As to the Teacher.	B. As to the Teaching.
I. The Preparation. i. Work. ii. Live.	I. The Students. i. Essentials. Ignorance and Intelligence. ii. Adaptation. Grading.
II. The Purpose. i. Essential. Spiritual Results. ii. Processional. Knowledge. Obedience.	II. The System. i. Occasions. Existing Organizations. ii. Apparatus. Eargate and Eyegate.
III. The Process. i. Persistence. ii. Patience.	III. The Scheme. i. Extensive. ii. Intensive.

IF it be accepted that the supreme responsibility of the Christian Church is that of the knowledge and incarnation of the truth of the Bible, in order that it may be proclaimed to the world, it will at once be recognized that the subject of her equipment for the fulfillment of this purpose is of the utmost importance. In considering the subject, therefore, of the method of the teaching of the English Bible we shall confine our attention to the true method as within the Church of God.

I do not mean to suggest that our teaching of the Bible will be confined exclusively to Christian people; but I am dealing with the method of the teaching of the Bible within the atmosphere of the Church, on Church premises, and in connection with the regular work of the Church.

Mr. D. L. Moody once said, "The Christian is the world's Bible, and very often a revised version is needed." I believe the whole of that statement to be true, but for the moment am particularly interested in the first part of it. The great truths of the Bible can only be communicated to the nation and to the world through the Church of God; but it cannot be too often repeated, and furthermore it must be remembered, that this communication of Bible truth to the world by the Church cannot be accomplished merely by proclamation. There must be a manifestation through the lives of those who constitute the Church, who, according to the prayer of the Divine Lord and Master, are sanctified through the truth. To leave these fundamental considerations out of any discussion of method in teaching would be to neglect a most important factor therein.

A glance at the diagram will reveal the outline of our subject. We shall deal with the subject of method first as to the teacher and, secondly, as to the teaching.

A. As to the Teacher

I. *The preparation.*

It is inevitable that when we deal with the subject of method we commence with the teacher; and the first matter of importance is that there should be adequate preparation for the work. In order to preparation two things are necessary, which may be briefly expressed in the words "work" and "live."

As to the first, let me state in the briefest manner possible what I want to impress upon the mind of those who are contemplating Bible teaching, by declaring that the Bible never yields itself to indolence. Of all literature none demands more diligent application than that of the Divine Library. To that statement let me hasten to add another. The Bible yields its treasures to honest toil more readily than does any other serious literature. No one can be a teacher of this Book who treats it with scant intellectual application and respect; but, on the other hand, those who devote to it earnest work according to their opportunity may become teachers in the best sense of the word.

Limitations which are fixed within the government of God are no barrier to preparation for teaching; but limitations which are created by the indolence of men constitute a barrier insurmountable.

I draw special attention to this fact because I am so often asked, "What method would you advise for a person who has very little time for study?" If a person has honestly very little time, but uses that time with all application, earnestness, and diligence, God will make up to such an one in ways which will be full of surprise. Only let none expect this Divine help unless there be honest and full use of whatever time or opportunity may be available.

To ministers and students preparing for the ministry I most definitely say that it is impossible to be teachers of the Word apart from hard, honest, and continuous sweat of brain in the sacred business of studying the Bible. No man can truly teach it who picks it up and reads it casually, and then, when some isolated passage has impressed him, lays it aside while he attempts to find on his bookshelves things which other men have said concerning the passage which has appealed to him. That is not study of the Bible, and it cannot issue in teaching of the Bible.

On the other hand, those occupied in business, whose hours are few and precious, but who make full use of those hours to the utmost of their ability, may expect and assuredly will find that God will give them such clear insight into the meaning of His Word, and such wonderful unveilings of its hidden glories, that they will be growingly amazed; for this Book is not as other books, as there is ever super-added to that wonderful and mystic quality of its own inspiration, an inspiration within the one who is earnestly devoted to the work of discovering its meaning. The human side of the literature may be appreciated and studied by the unaided intellect of man; but the Divine element, that which constitutes it, inspired literature, demands that the student shall be inspired, and this inspiration is given only to those who dedicate their best strength to the work of studying the writings.

The work of preparation involves familiarity with the familiar things, accompanied by determination to become familiar with the familiar things. Does that sound like a paradox? Think of it. There are some things with which we are so familiar that we do not know them. We know them by rote; we know them by hearsay; we know them by the habit of continuously repeating them; but some of these most familiar things we do not know, never having come to a true apprehension of their significance. It is important, therefore, that we begin on the simplest level with the determination to give attention to those fundamental matters with which we dealt in our first lecture, and to make ourselves intelligent possessors of them for all time.

Let the Bible teacher make use of all available means to help him in his study of the Bible. When I earnestly plead for the reading of the Bible itself, I am sometimes asked, "Do you suggest that a man should burn all the books he has about the Bible?" or, "Do you say that a man should never procure any book about the Bible?" Certainly I mean nothing of the kind, and earnestly advise whomsoever may contemplate the work of teaching to secure every available aid.

To young people I would, however, say, even if you have the means, do not buy a library of expository works. Build up your own library one book at a time, according to that particular portion of the Bible which you are studying. Select and choose, under the advice of those in whom you have most confidence, the books you require; and buying and studying them one at a time, you will presently find that you have gathered around you familiar friends in your books. Such a collection constitutes a true library. It is quite true that you can buy at cheap and reduced rates whole series of commentaries, but the probability is that if you do so the majority of them will never help you; but the books which you gather one by one will certainly be those of greatest value to you throughout the whole course of your ministry of teaching.

The second word indicating the true method of preparation is the word "live." If it be true that the Bible never yields itself to indolence, it is equally true that it never yields itself to disobedience; and also that it does yield up its secrets growingly to honest obedience.

There never can be weight and point and power in teaching unless the mystic and spiritual truths which have come to us as the result of our study are obeyed.

And in this connection let me say that there never can be the study of any part of the Divine Library, but that there will come from such study some definite and direct appeal.

The Divine Library is a revelation, and a revelation means light, and light means an unveiling of the things of darkness, accompanied by a demand that they should be put away.

We cannot study the story of the men of the past, with its account of earnest purpose and constant conflict in the struggle after the high and noble in the mere twilight of revelation, and with its revelation of the principle of faith that made them strong and courageous, without being conscious of the lure of that life. When that consciousness is felt, there must be not merely the intellectual apprehension of the truth, but the answer of the will thereto. Where we fail in this respect, the Bible immediately becomes a sealed book.

It is impossible to read the stories of the past without discovering the reason of the failure of certain men ; and that quality of the revelation is in itself a flaming light of warning falling upon our own lives; but if we persist in the things against which we are warned, the Bible becomes a sealed book, and we can neither know it, nor teach it.

This is a mystic quality constituting a difference between the Bible and all other literature. I may study Shakespeare, and the tragedy of "Macbeth" breaking in upon my soul, I may see the awfulness of sin, and yet may fall a prey to the same sin without losing my ability to take up another of the writings of Shakespeare, and to understand its teaching. But if I read the story of wrong in the Bible, and do not yield to the teaching conveyed thereby, I cannot take up another part of the Bible and understand it on its highest spiritual level.

I am sometimes asked if I do not think that what is known as Higher Criticism has hindered people from reading the Bible. Well, that may be so; but I am quite convinced that people have far more often been hindered by their own disobedience to the Bible, because by such disobedience the eye becomes dim and the ear dull.

All that is supremely true in the case of the teacher. We, who in preparation for teaching must necessarily deal with the technicalities, will become sounding brass, tinkling cymbals, the click of the machinery forever discoverable in our very method, save as our teaching is rendered powerful by conformity of life to the claim which the Bible sets up thereupon. There is nothing more disastrous than to traffic with the letter of Scripture while we disobey its spirit. By such action we become such as having eyes, see not; having ears, hear not; and therefore are unable to communicate to others the virtue and glory of the revelation of God.

These are solemn words, but full of importance. The Bible teacher must remember that the twofold preparation necessary is that of hard work and consistent life.

II. *The purpose.*

The teacher of the Bible must ever have in mind the twofold purpose of the work, what I may describe as the essential and the processional.

As to the essential, I take it for granted that we accept the preliminary considerations that the Bible is religious, that it is dual, triple, multiple, and unified. I take it for granted, moreover, that we have not only accepted these things, but have come to the conclusion that the unified message of the Bible is a full and final revelation to men, for the purposes of the present life, concerning spiritual things. Consequently we are face to face in Bible literature with the deepest values of human life.

It is a literature with a purpose, and *that purpose is spiritual.* It is a literature intended to bring men into the knowledge of God, and into direct dealing with God. It is a literature intended to teach men what God is, what man is, and what the interrelationships between God and men are. It is a literature intended to set sin in its right light, that men may shun it; and to reveal to men all the high and the noble things of their essential spiritual nature.

We must remember, therefore, whenever we teach, that the ultimate purpose of our teaching is not the illumination of the intellect; is not the moving of the emotion; but is the bringing of the lives of the people who hear, and understand, into right relationship with eternal things.

That is why no man can teach the Bible unless he himself be a spiritual man. That is why—let me say it almost with bated breath, and yet with strong conviction—I object to the teaching of the English Bible in State schools by teachers about whose spiritual life I am not sure, and into the condition of which I have no right to investigate. I believe in the Bible being read in the schools of the nation; but I hold that it should be read without note or comment, because we cannot investigate, and we ought not to investigate, as to the spiritual character or religious convictions of the teachers in State schools. We are in constant peril when we ask men to teach or interpret the Bible, save as they are called and prepared by God for that sacred and solemn work.

The processional purpose must also be recognized. In teaching the Bible our first business is to impart knowledge, to make others see, to be perfectly sure that the people we are teaching understand—whether there be a multitude or half a dozen matters nothing. That is teaching.

In teaching we must be prepared to sacrifice many things held in high esteem, such as dignity of deportment and beauty of style. I am convinced that in order to teach the Bible we must be free from slavery to a perfected style, and I am absolutely certain we must be emancipated from the bondage of dignity. The business of the teacher is to teach, and that means that his supreme anxiety must be that of enabling those whom he is teaching to see the things he sees.

I am not undervaluing beauty of style or dignity of deportment, but I do desire to make it perfectly clear that in the teaching of the Bible these are secondary things, the frame rather than the picture, and I would rather sacrifice the frame to the picture than the picture to the frame.

Then, again, processionally our purpose must be that of leading those whom we teach to obedience. Whether they are pleased or pained by the truth presented is always a secondary matter, or, rather, it ought to have no place in our consideration. Moreover, the supreme matter is not the theory, but the practice which grows out of the theory, and our work as Bible teachers is never completed when we have merely instructed the intelligence or moved the emotion. There must be superadded to these, that note of appeal, which was always found in the prophetic utterances of the old economy, and is persistent in the apostolic teaching of the new.

III. *The process.*

Finally, the teacher of the Bible must follow a twofold process, which may again be described by two words—"persistence" and "patience."

By persistence I mean constant repetition. It was Dr. Dale, of Birmingham, who once told a meeting of ministers that they might expect people to understand what they meant when they had repeated it ten times. Personally, I am not sure that ten times is enough for the average man. When I began the work of more definitely teaching the Bible the thing that troubled me was that in teaching it was necessary to repeat, and perhaps there is no phantom that fills the soul of the young preacher with more horror than that of repeating himself, and that may be a perfectly healthy fear; but he need have no fear of repeating the Word of God. In this connection the words of Paul have been to me a source of great comfort—"To write the same things to you, to me indeed is not irksome; but for you it is safe." That is the doctrine of repetition, and that is what I mean when I speak of persistence.

But it is absolutely necessary that we understand that persistence involves patience. Do not let any Bible teacher expect too much at first from his students. Let him remember the slowness of his own apprehension, and by the memory be made patient with the slowness of those whom he is teaching. I was recently asked if I did not consider that it was time that I should cease work at Westminster, because people who had been attending the Bible School for six years ought now to be fully instructed as to the general content of Bible books. I very much doubt whether those who have attended through the whole period can be considered as fully instructed, both on account of the imperfection of the teaching, and the slowness with which men apprehend great themes.

Finally, strengthen your persistence and your patience by remembering that the Bible teacher cannot and ought not to do everything. Leave something for the student to do. Be content to leave your theme unfinished; for the true system of education is not that of cramming, but that of suggesting, so that the mind may act for itself and, proceeding along the line indicated, grasp the larger meaning and the final truth.

B. As to the Teaching

I. *The students.*

In actual teaching the matter of first importance is that of the students, and it is of supreme importance that the teacher should remember two things concerning them, which we may describe as: essential facts, and the need for adaptation.

As to the essentials, they are those of their ignorance and intelligence. The teacher of the Bible must remember that nothing must be taken for granted as to the knowledge of the students, and that their capacity for knowledge must be taken for granted in every case. I think teachers often make mistakes along each of these lines. They imagine that people know simple things which they do not really know; and, secondly, they imagine that people are not equal to grasping what they have to teach. We need to rid ourselves of these two false assumptions. We should face our students, taking nothing for granted, but determined to be simple and elementary in order to reach the level of the most simple mind; but at the same time believing that that simplest mind is capable of grasping the profoundest truth we are able to teach. Our business is to state the truth in the simplest way possible, but never to shrink from communicating what appeals to us as a profound truth, because we imagine that those whom we teach are not able to comprehend it.

I was greatly impressed five-and-twenty years ago by reading advice which Mr. Spurgeon gave to young preachers, when he told them that having made a sermon which they considered to be above the average, they were not to save it because the next occasion on which they were to preach was not in their opinion a great occasion. He charged them to preach the best they had, whenever they stood up to face a congregation. That, I believe, is a principle of supreme importance. Then let us take nothing for granted, except the ignorance and intelligence of those whom we teach.

In dealing with students it is of perpetual importance that there should be adaptation. To-day this is being emphasized in the work of our Sunday-schools by insistence upon the necessity for grading the children. It is of equal importance, so far as it is possible under the more difficult circumstances of mixed congregations, that the teacher should gauge the mental capacity of his audience, not as to the truth he has to teach, that he finds in his Bible, but as to the method by which he imparts the truth, as to the language he employs, as to the illustrations he uses.

It may be that the ability to do that is either the final acquirement or the specific gift of the true teacher. To be able to confront an audience, and immediately to detect the general level of its ability to follow, and to be able therefore to adapt oneself in the use of language and illustration, so as to convey essential truth to that audience, is the supreme quality of great teaching. To be able to speak the same truth here, with illustrations which would not be understood there ; and there, to declare the truth in a way which would not be apprehended here ; the truth always the same, but the method differing—that gift, I am inclined to think, cannot be imparted by any school of pedagogy, but it can be imparted by the Spirit of God ; and we may pray that in that way we may be made apt to teach. I am convinced that persons who seem to lack that ability can receive it in wonderful fashion by the preparation of the Spirit of God.

II. *The system.*

When in dealing with the teaching of the Bible we turn from the students to the system we are compelled to become more than ever technical, and therefore we may deal with the subject in the briefest way possible. There are again two things to be borne in mind—occasions and apparatus.

As to occasions, I am often asked by my brethren in the ministry, "Where shall we adopt these methods of Bible teaching?" I would reply to all such enquiry, that the first thing is to capture existing organizations for Bible teaching. Let us see to it first of all that our Sunday-schools are Bible schools, and if the International Lesson system is calculated to help you, use it, and if not, abandon it. Especially would I emphasize the importance of real Bible study among the elder scholars in our schools, those which under the new organization are gathered into the Institute department. Do not let us make the mistake of imagining that the Bible will not interest them. Nothing has been more definitely vindicated in my own experience than the fact that our young people are supremely interested in systematic teaching of the Scriptures. To-day the most attractive thing in our work among young people, judged by their attendance, is not the recreation section, is not the intellectual section, of great importance as we hold these both to be, but it is the study of the Bible carefully and systematically, under trained teachers, in separate classes on Sunday afternoons.

I repeat that in order to teach the Bible in the life of our Church we need to capture the existing organizations. If I could have my way, I would make it a rule that the week-night service should be everywhere turned into a Bible school, where the Bible is taught patiently, persistently, and consecutively.

As to the apparatus, let me cover the whole ground by saying that in Bunyan's allegory of the capture of Mansoul he has revealed a matter of supreme importance by his emphasis upon the fact that eyegate is of equal value with eargate in gaining access to the central citadel of personality. In our teaching let us make use of diagrams and charts, and blackboards, and anything else which will give those whom we desire to teach the opportunity of the vision as well as the voice, and thus lead them to an apprehension of the truths of the Bible.

I pass over this question of apparatus quite briefly because teachers must make use of whatever aids will be of most service to them in the doing of their work.

III. *The scheme.*

The final matter as to teaching is that of the scheme, and the ground may be covered by saying that the scheme of Bible teaching should be extensive and intensive.

The extensive is always the first method. If I desired to teach a child geography, I should first take it to the globe, and let it turn it about with its own fingers, while I showed land and water, and indicated facts suggested by the pictures, afterwards crystallizing them into definitions. To begin with a book in which words such as "peninsula" and "isthmus" are printed, without allowing them to see Italy or Panama, is not to succeed in helping them to understand. Then, still with the globe before them, I would tell them stories of the countries. From that general impression I would pass to outline maps of separate countries, and thus gradually approach the intensive method of full maps and text-books.

All which is a parable illustrative of the true method with the Bible. We must begin with extensive work, with broad outlines, with analyses. An analysis is the separation of a compound into its constituent parts. For instance: Water = Oxygen + Hydrogen. That is analysis. Synthesis is the uniting of elements into a compound. For instance: Hydrogen + Oxygen = Water. That is synthesis. Thus we go over the books in analysis, and say the Gospel of the King presents His Person, His Propaganda, His Passion. That is analysis.

And again we say, the Person by His Propaganda and His Passion is King. That is synthesis. Those who have followed this method will find the value when they turn to intensive work, when they ponder the parts, and weigh the words, and are determined not to rest until they have found the deepest meaning.

Let me close this lecture and this brief series by declaring that Bible teaching is the supreme work of the Christian ministry, and the supreme work of the Sunday-school teacher. Let Christian ministers and Sunday-school teachers devote themselves to this work, and the result will be the Bible known and lived by the Church of God; and that will mean purity and compassion, living and active, in the affairs of men. Only so will the nation receive that Word of God, without which its conceptions will be vulgar, its conduct debased, and its character degraded.

So may we all, in the measure open to us, be teachers of the Word—hearers, doers, and teachers—helping thus to meet the need of the Church and the need of the world at large.